American History

Y. kids

American History 1

Copyright © 2005 Sam & Youngjin Singapore Pte, Ltd.

World rights reserved. No part of this publication may be stored in a retrieval system, transmitted, or reproduced in any way, including but not limited to photocopy, photograph, magnetic, or other record, without the prior agreement and written permission of the publisher.

ISBN: 981-05-2765-9

Printed in the Republic of Korea.

Distributed by Publishers Group West.

How to contact us

E-mail: feedback@youngjin.com.sg

Address: Youngjin Singapore Pte, Ltd.
70 Anson Road, #22-04, Apex Tower
Singapore 079905

Telephone: +65 - 6327 -1161
Fax: +65 - 6327 -1151

Manager: Suzie Lee
Production Editor: Cris Lee
Editorial Supervisor: John Song Lee
Copyeditor: Elisabeth Beller
Proofreaders: Elisabeth Beller, Rand Miranda

Story: Allen Kim
Art: Nicole Kim
Color: Winsorblue

Book Designer: Litmus
Cover Designer: Litmus

American History

Vol 1

sam

Story | Allen Kim
Art | Nicole Kim
Color | Winsorblue

Y. kids

To Teachers and Parents

Who were the people who made the adventurous journey across the Bering Sea and into what is know today as Alaska?

Who were the Europeans who first landed on North America?

Who were the Pilgrims who sailed on the Mayflower to the new continent?

What were their experiences like during the crossing and with settling this new land?

In this book, you will learn how the Pilgrim survived the bitterly cold winters by learning from the Native Americans how to cultivate corn and how to build a trade base for fur and wood.

You will also learn about the Puritans and why they moved to the new world to avoid religion oppression in Europe.

Also featured in this book are

★ Conflicts between the settlers and Native Americans.

★ The introduction of slavery to America.

★ The society, education and culture of the new continent in the 17th century

★ The Colonial government, its conflicts with the British and the circumstances that led to the Declaration of Independence and the Revolutionary War.

Contents

American History 1

EPISODE 1: The First Americans

The last Ice Age on Earth was at its height from 34,000 to 30,000 BC.

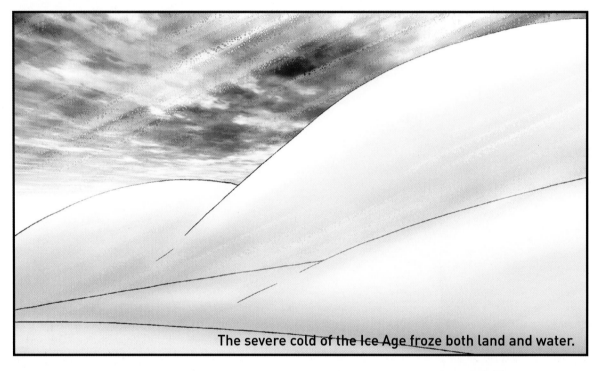

The severe cold of the Ice Age froze both land and water.

Less and less water ran into the sea, so the sea during this Ice Age—even at its highest level—was about five inches *lower* than it is now.

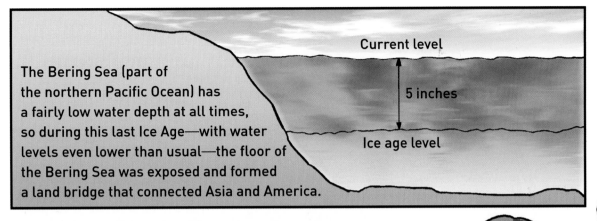

The Bering Sea (part of the northern Pacific Ocean) has a fairly low water depth at all times, so during this last Ice Age—with water levels even lower than usual—the floor of the Bering Sea was exposed and formed a land bridge that connected Asia and America.

Current level

5 inches

Ice age level

At its peak, the land bridge was some 930 miles wide.

The land bridge was covered with plants, such as grasses and mosses, and this brought many animals to feed there.

And the animals, in turn, attracted the first humans who were searching for animals to hunt.

These people—the first to step into North America, perhaps while hunting animals for their survival—probably had no idea that they had just discovered a new continent.

Arriving in what is now Alaska, the first people to come to the new continent moved south.

It may have taken thousands of years for them to arrive in what is now the continental United States.

A hunting shelter dating back to about 12,000 BC was recently discovered in Alaska.

Evidence that proves they lived in North America during this period continues to be found even today.

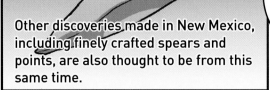

Other discoveries made in New Mexico, including finely crafted spears and points, are also thought to be from this same time.

Native Americans lived for several thousand years isolated from other civilizations until the Europeans arrived.

At the time that Columbus came to the "New World," it is estimated that there were about 50 million Native Americans in the American continents.

Of those, only about 1.5 to 2 million Native Americans lived in the area that is now the United States.

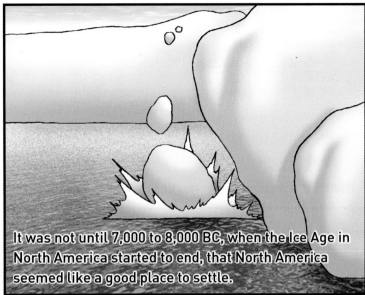

It was not until 7,000 to 8,000 BC, when the Ice Age in North America started to end, that North America seemed like a good place to settle.

Before that, most Native Americans lived in the southern areas because the warmer climate offered a friendlier environment. They flourished in what is now Mexico and Peru, and they founded the amazing Incan and Mayan civilizations.

The Native Americans in North America did not have this sort of civilization.

Up until the 1500s, most Native Americans in what is now the United States were dependent on a mix of farming and hunting for their survival. Only the Anasazi, who lived in what is now New Mexico and Arizona, built houses for a longer stay.

Native Americans on the prairies continued to rely on hunting for survival, constantly moving to follow herds of buffalo.

They used only bows and spears as they walked.

Most Native Americans in the eastern United States relied on farming for their survival.

They also hunted animals (such as deer) or went out in canoes to catch fish.

They sometimes wore clothes made of skins of the beavers they hunted.

Of all Native Americans, those who lived in the Pacific Northwest were the most well-off because they had plenty of food supplies, such as fish.

Native Americans formed tribes, and each was led by a chief or older member of the tribe. The chiefs were strong leaders to their people.

The culture of the different tribes were passed on by the telling of tales and myths.

The First Americans

A long time ago, the present Gobi Desert in Central Asia was a blessed land with widespread meadows and fertile fields. Then, one day, sudden coldness came to this mild land. Because of the coldness, the Earth began to dry up and the animals on the meadows began to disappear.

Those who had lived comfortable lives for a long time had to leave for a new land to survive. A much more sterile and cold land was waiting for them who left for new lives. But they adjusted themselves to the new environment, and then they went to Siberia and the Bering Sea where they could walk on its bottom. After reaching what is now Alaska, they kept on going to the south, and finally they could live widespread in North and South America of today.

Though this story is the one which was formed by the imagination, most scholars think that the American aborigines moved from Central Asia to Siberia, Alaska and then to American continent.

Indian Culture

The Indian society was very simple. There were neither ruling classes like kings or the aristocracy nor low classes like slaves or the low-class people in their society. They respected the old, loved children and understood and loved nature.

The Indian society was led by the chieftain or the elder. They became judges and advisors in case of tribal conflicts. They decided important matters including not only tribal interior matters but also the intertribal relations. Their authority was quite powerful and the their people followed their decisions willingly.

EPISODE 2: Europe Meets the New World

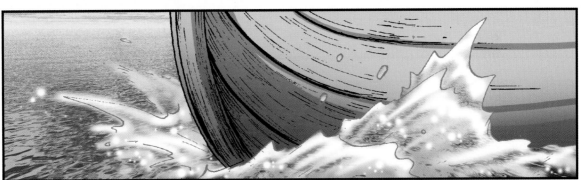

The first Known European to arrive in North America was Lief Eriksson, a Norseman from Greenland.

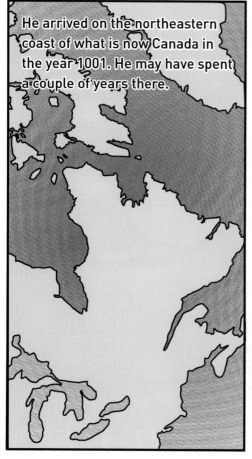

He arrived on the northeastern coast of what is now Canada in the year 1001. He may have spent a couple of years there.

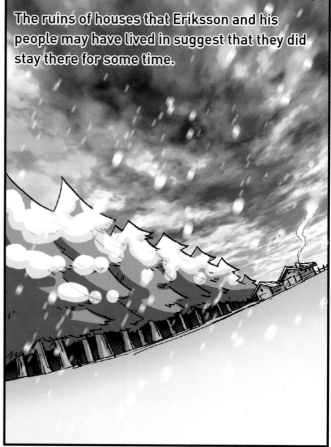

The ruins of houses that Eriksson and his people may have lived in suggest that they did stay there for some time.

These ruins were discovered in northern Newfoundland in 1963.

Yet their discovery did not have much of an impact on the rest of the world.

It was not until several centuries after Eriksson's discovery—On August 3, 1492—that Christopher Columbus, with the help of Queen Isabella of Spain, launched his voyage into the Atlantic, along with 90 sailors on three ships.

Columbus

My goal is to find a westward sea route to India and China.

They say the Earth is round. So when I go to the West, I should eventually arrive in India.

That must be India over there!

On October 12, 1492, sixty-nine days after they left...

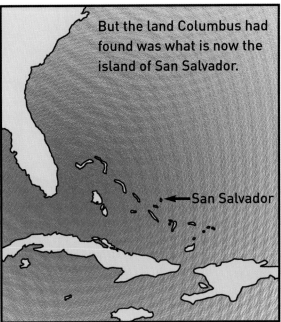

But the land Columbus had found was what is now the island of San Salvador.

San Salvador

Columbus' voyage shocked Europe.

I thought there was a waterfall at the end of the world!

Then is it really true that the Earth is round?

In those days, few believed that the Earth was round. This new fact served as a starting point for a time of travel across the Atlantic Ocean.

In 1497, five years after Columbus' discovery of San Salvador, a Venetian sailor named John Cabot arrived in North America at Newfoundland with support from Britain.

Cabot's journey opened the way to the world's largest fishing area, called George's Banks.

Wow! This sea is full of fish!

Cabot's accomplishment didn't get much attention at that time, but it was later used by the British to claim North America as their own.

In those days, Spain was the leader of exploring the American continent.

In 1513, a Spanish exploration group led by Juan Ponce de Leon landed on the Florida coast near where St. Augustine is today.

Spain conquered Mexico in 1522, further strengthening Spain's powerful position in North America.

In 1539, a Spanish expedition under Hernando de Soto explored the southeastern area from what is now Florida to the Mississippi River.

In 1540, another Spaniard, Francisco de Coronado, arrived.

My goal is to find the mythical Seven Cities of Cibola.

If I could only find that land full of gold and treasure.

Muhahahaha!

Then I'd be the richest man in the world!

Coronado traveled to the Grand Canyon and Kansas in search of the gold and treasure, but he didn't find any.

During the expedition, Coronado and his men lost some of the horses they had brought from Spain.

The escaped horses survived on the plains, and their numbers grew.

After a while, Native Americans started to catch the horses to tame and ride them.

Meanwhile, in 1532, France sent Jacques Cartier to explore the St. Lawrence River.

This was later a basis for French claims to North America. Britain also sent expedition groups led by Humphrey Gilbert and Walter Raleigh.

In 1587, the first British immigrants tried to settle on Roanoke Island off the coast of North Carolina...

...but they failed.

The settlement was tried again two years later, but it also failed. Finally, on April 6, 1607, a group of settlers set out for the Chesapeake Bay and set up a British colony there. That colony was called Jamestown.

EPISODE 3: Early Settlements

In the battle on the sea in 1588 between Spain's "Invincible Armada" and British ships, the British had a great victory.

This gave the British great freedom to travel on the Atlantic Ocean...

...and encouraged many Europeans to move North America.

Before this time, Spain, using the power of its armada, tried to keep other countries from moving to the New World.

But the trip to the New World was nothing but hardship.

Immigrants had to cross the Atlantic in small, crowded ships.

It usually took them seven to twelve weeks to arrive in the New World—sometimes even longer.

Because they were low on supplies, many immigrants died of diseases before they even landed, and ships were often lost at sea because of storms.

Despite the hardships of the journey, people continued to come to the New World continued. Many of those immigrants in the early 1600s were Puritans, also known as Pilgrims.

One group of Puritans had originally moved to the Netherlands to avoid oppression in Britain. But there were other problems there.

So, they returned to Britain to get approval from the Virginia Company to own land in the New World, and they set sail on a ship called the Mayflower.

But the ship was hit by a storm on its way to the New World.

It was forced off course and arrived at Cape Cod on November 11, 1620, far north of the land they had arranged to live on.

Finally!
We're in the New World!
Let's get off the ship.

Wait!
We've got something to do before we land.

What's that?

It's very important!

?

?

This is not the land we had a contract for with the Virginia Company.

No, it's not. We're far north from it.

So this place is not under the rule of the British government.

In this way, the Mayflower's passengers agreed to work together to make a community based on religious freedom and equality, and then they elected John Carver as their governor. The agreement that was worked out that day was called the Mayflower Compact.

A series of painful troubles awaited the hopeful Pilgrims.

Almost half of them died of the severe cold and lack of food during the first winter they spent there.

They had strong wills and religious beliefs. They survived the troubles and no one got back on board the Mayflower when the ship returned to Britain the next year.

They survived largely because of the help of the neighboring Wampanoag Native American tribe who taught them how to grow corn.

Thanks to the Native Americans, the pilgrims were able to harvest a very good crop of corn...

...and they didn't have to worry about food shortages any longer.

Later, the Pilgrims invited the Native Americans to a feast to celebrate a great harvest and also to show their thanks for what the Native Americans had done for them. This feast is the origin of Thanksgiving.

The Pilgrims slowly got used to the land as time went by.

The town called Plymouth that they built remained almost completely self-governed and independent until Massachusetts claimed it some time later.

Following the settlement made by the Pilgrims, several other British colonies were created along the northeastern coast of North America.

The pioneer spirit, strong will and passion for religions freedom made a foundation for what was to become the United States.

Immigrants at the Early Stage

The Mayflower was a medium-sized sailing boat with three sails.
The immigrants at the early stage came to the new continent by such small boats through the violent waves of the Atlantic Ocean and their navigations were very perilous.
What the immigrants, who arrived in the new continent for better lives, had to do first was securing food and shelter.

First, they cut trees to build their cottages. And then they reclaimed the land clutivated the fields for farming.

Their lives were followed by continuous hardships.
Many people died of deficient food, extreme cold and Indian attacks.
The fact that almost half of the Pilgrim fathers who came there by the Mayflower died within one year is evidence of the difficulty.
However, they succeeded in overcoming all of difficulties with strong will and courage, and they became the root of today's America.

The ships that navigated the Atlantic Ocean

Columbus' Santa Maria

The Mayflower of Pilgrim fathers

Luxurious passenger boats of today

EPISODE 4: Immigrants and Native Americans

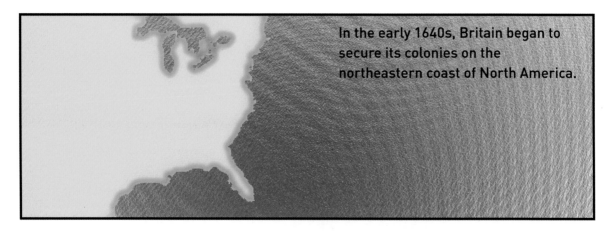

In the early 1640s, Britain began to secure its colonies on the northeastern coast of North America.

Native Americans lived inland from the coast and they were no strangers to the settlers in the East.

At this time, the immigrant settlers and the Native Americans were friendly to each other.

We've learned some skills and made profits by trading with these people.

We've gotten a lot of help from the first settlers of Jamestown and from the Pilgrims in Plymouth.

But the new settlers are...

The good lands were all taken by other settlers before we got to them.

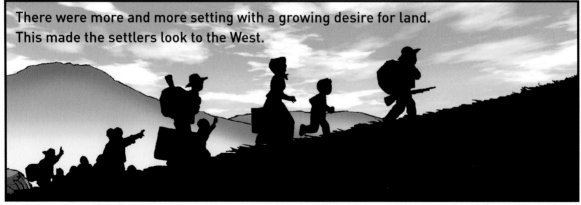

There were more and more setting with a growing desire for land.
This made the settlers look to the West.

Eventually this led to fights with Native Americans.

The traditional weapons of Native Americans were no match for the modern weapons of the settlers.

Some Native American tribes were united in a strong and organized resistance to the immigrant settlers.

But even united, they were not strong enough to stop the wave of the settlers who forced the Native Americans more and more to the West.

13 Colonies

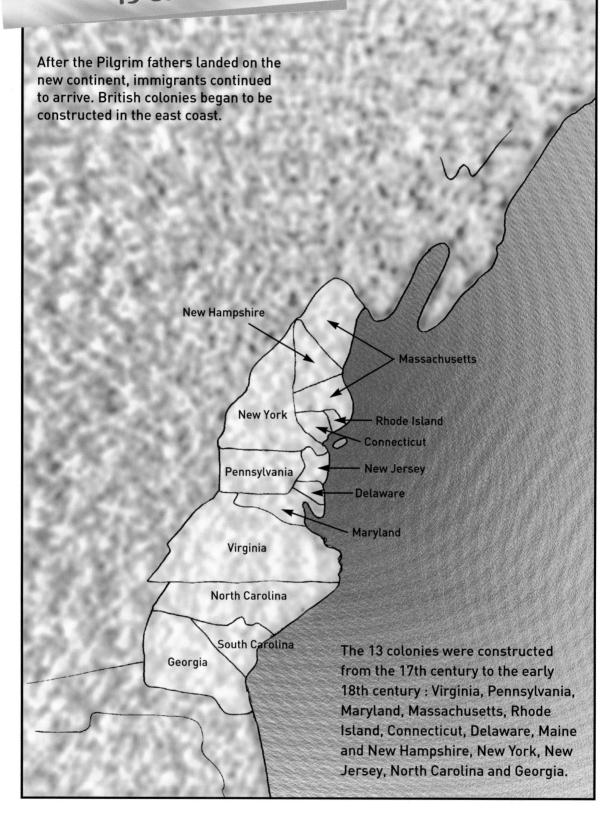

After the Pilgrim fathers landed on the new continent, immigrants continued to arrive. British colonies began to be constructed in the east coast.

New Hampshire

Massachusetts

New York

Rhode Island

Connecticut

Pennsylvania

New Jersey

Delaware

Maryland

Virginia

North Carolina

South Carolina

Georgia

The 13 colonies were constructed from the 17th century to the early 18th century : Virginia, Pennsylvania, Maryland, Massachusetts, Rhode Island, Connecticut, Delaware, Maine and New Hampshire, New York, New Jersey, North Carolina and Georgia.

Indians vs Immigrants

When the immigrants first landed on the new continent the Indians didn't feel threatened. The number of the immigrants was not so large, so their territories didn't overlap and little risk of conflict existed.

The Indians benefited in the trade with the immigrants. They purchased such products as knives, axes, weapons and fishing hooks, and they were used significantly and they could also stand at an advantageous position in competing with other tribes. But as the number of the immigrants increased day by day, conflicts were inevitable. The relations between the Indians and the immigrants at the early stage can be described as the uneasy relations in which cooperation and conflict were mixed together.

EPISODE 5:
The Full-Scale Immigration of Europeans

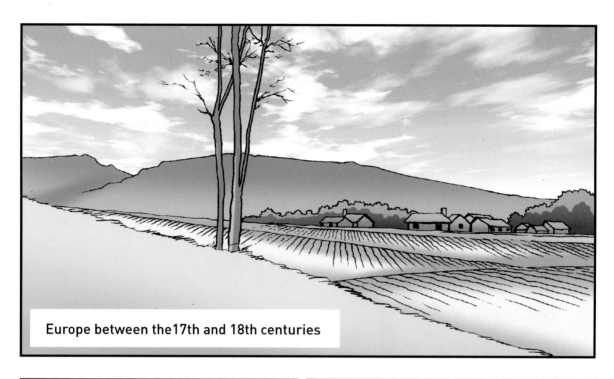

Europe between the 17th and 18th centuries

Not long after Columbus discovered it, the American continent turned into a great attraction for many people.

What brought all these people to the American continent?

Leaving their beloved families, friends and everything they had built was not easy.

But some had to leave before they starved to death.

No matter how hard they worked, living in Europe was extremely difficult for ordinary people.

The wealthiest people owned almost all the land.

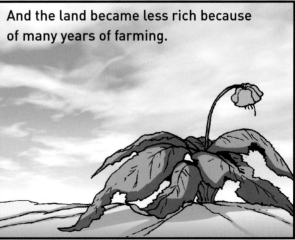

And the land became less rich because of many years of farming.

But there was a lot of land for anyone in the America, and the soil there was rich. The weather was perfect for farming, too.

In America, anyone can own this fertile land.

The American continent had some of the best land for growing food.

Its rivers and sea were rich with food.

The vast plains were good for cattle.

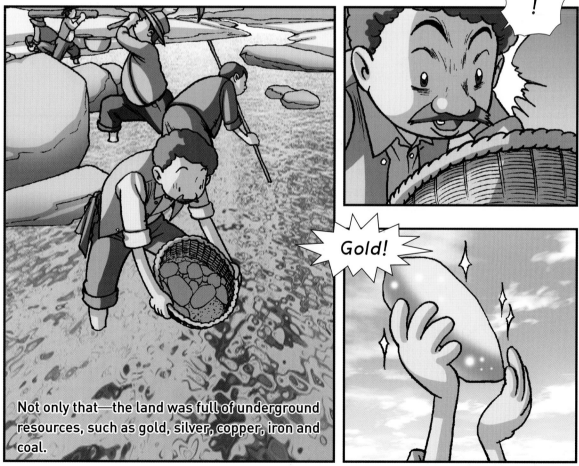

!

Gold!

Not only that—the land was full of underground resources, such as gold, silver, copper, iron and coal.

Pay in Europe was very low because there were many more workers than jobs.

But pay in America was high because there was so much work to be done and too few workers.

For these reasons, more and more workers came to America.

More workers meant greater need for houses, bridges, roads, clothes and other things needed for living.

To meet these new needs, America needed even more workers. This encouraged even more people who needed jobs to come to America.

People also migrated to avoid the religious oppression in their homelands.

In those days, European religious conflicts were a growing problem, and many were not generous about accepting different religions.

But in America, people could practice any religion they wanted.

People also moved to America for political reasons.

Europeans could be harsh with those who had different political views.

But America wasn't.

We can say and write and argue whatever we want.

If our belief is not allowed here, we can simply move to another colony.

Every colony tries so hard to attract more people.

For all of these reasons, more and more people moved to America.

In the early 1500s, hundreds of immigrants started their life in the New World.
By 1690 its population reached 250,000.
And this figure grew to more than 2,500,000 by 1775.

Let's go to the Land of Freedom

The difficulties which the early immigrants had to experience were not so easy to overcome: Perilous sailing routes against violent waves and typhoons, sterile soil and coldness, and hunger and fights against violent natives.

Despite these inferior conditions, lots of people came to the new continent.

What made them come to this land?
What was the reason why they came to the new continent leaving behind their beloved hometowns and friends?

Freedom! It was the freedom!

Freedom from hunger and poverty, freedom from oppressions and tedious wars, and freedom from discrimination and corrupt society. Those were the reasons why they came to America.

Accordingly, they were not the aristocracy in Europe, and their spirit toward freedom became the most important factor which made America of today.

I Protect My Land

Though they had to experience many difficulties to settle there successfully, the new continent was a land of freedom and unlimited opportunity.

Most people were living in their settlement along the coast, and lots of unoccupied lands were waiting for them if they went to the west for a day or two.

But they had to pay the cost to protect freedom. They had to fight against unexpected native attacks and the government's illegal assertion of ownership which intended to deprive them of the land they reclaimed with difficulty.

To them, freedom was their lands and their lives. To protect their land, they took up weapons, and they believed firmly that they have to take up weapons to protect them from invaders. This fact became the basis of accepting the right to possess weapons in their Constitution later.

EPISODE 6: The Economy and Culture of the New World

What frist caught the attention of the settlers was the vast unowned land of the New World.

This is it! This will be enough to support my family!

They worked hard and began to settle in the New World.

Those who arrived earliest took the good land near the coast and were the lucky ones.

...and stone-covered land.

This place has nothing but dense forest...

The latecomers were not that lucky.

Ouch!

First they cut down trees to build huts.

Then they took stones out of the ground so they could farm.

Even fighting severe cold, food shortages and physical hardships, they survived.

Several bad experiences made the settlers stronger and more independent.

They came to feel strongly attached to the land that they had spent their lives to make usable.

The efforts of the settlers slowly turned the barren land into a good place to live.

How else can I make money?

As their lives stabilized, the settlers started to look for something else.

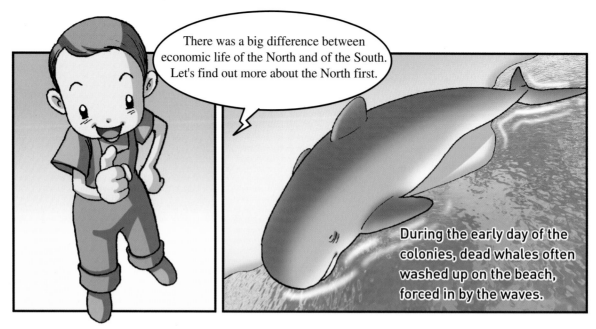

There was a big difference between economic life of the North and of the South. Let's find out more about the North first.

During the early day of the colonies, dead whales often washed up on the beach, forced in by the waves.

Gosh! What luck!

In those days, whale oil was highly prized as the best lamp fuel.

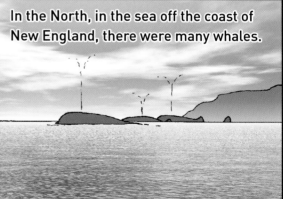

In the North, in the sea off the coast of New England, there were many whales.

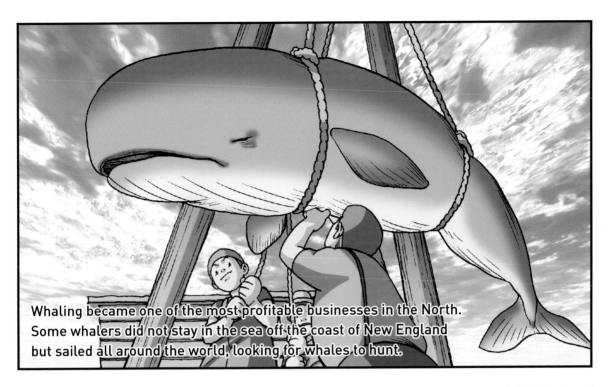

Whaling became one of the most profitable businesses in the North.
Some whalers did not stay in the sea off the coast of New England
but sailed all around the world, looking for whales to hunt.

Northerners also looked to Newfoundland, the world's largest fishing ground.

Fish they caught there was imported to Europe and the West Indies.

Also, there were large forests in the North.

Northerners were able to build ships at the cheapest price thanks to all the wood from the rich forest and soon the ship-building industry was very successful.

Meanwhile, smuggling also did very well in the North.

The British government strictly regulated the smuggling, but rhe merchants could not just give up the profitable business.

Sometimes rum made in America was shipped to Africa where a couple of bottles of rum was the price for one slave.

Slaves were then taken to the West Indies where they were sold to plantation owners.

Molasses—from which rum is made was purchased— in the West Indies and sold to the rum makers in America.

Ports in New York and Boston began flourish, and more and more people came to those cities that had ports.

Tobacco was the most popular farm product in the South, followed by rice and plants that could be used for dying cloth.

Cotton plantations weren't started until much later in the history of the South.

Instead of the forests of the North, which naturally made farming its main business.

Most crops grown in the South were exported (that is, sold to people outside of the South).

The biggest planters held most of the political power in the Southern colonies.

They lived in large, luxurious houses and threw big parties.

Their clothes and jewels and even furniture were imported(that is, made in other places and shipped to the South).

Unlike these wealthy farmers, small farmers and laborers in the South had to work very hard and were very poor. And the living conditions for the slaves were even worse.

The wealthy planters brought private teachers from Ireland or Scotland to teach their children or they sent their children to Britain to study.

Unlike the South, the North contained cities in which economic differences were not as great.

Also, there was more social equality in the North than in the South.

Tobacco Plant Farming

The early immigrants landed, settled and led their lives in different areas in different times respectively. By the way, differently from the North, the South had ideal agricultural backgrounds with wide lands and fertile fields.

The major industry of the South was growing tobacco plant.

Because there were lots of demand for tobacco plant in Europe, every product they grew was sold by them. Thus the southerners gained much profit by tobacco plant farming.
But there was a fatal weakness in tobacco plant farming.
The tobacco plants sterilized the soil quickly, so they couldn't farm them any longer on the land where tobacco plants had been grown for about three years. At that time, people didn't use fertilizer and they didn't know of discontinuous cultivation.

Therefore, in order to continue to grow tobacco plants, more new lands were needed and thus much more new lands were reclaimed.
By the result, farms got to become larger and more workers were needed.
The farms which had many workers could buy more lands,
and then reclaimed them, and accordingly they could gain much profit. Thus they continued to buy many small-sized farms.

The South became a society which is led by the owners of prosperous grand farms.

Whale Hunting

At the time when electricity was not invented, lighting was a very serious problem.
At that time, the whale oil candle which was made of the sperm whale oil came into the spotlight as the best lighting material.

As the candle burned much better than other lighting materials and its light was very bright with less soot, there were lots of demand for it in the high-class society.

The New Englanders didn't miss the fact that there were lots of sperm whales in front of their towns. They turned their sights to whale hunting and began to catch the whales. And soon after all the whales disappeared, they went about the seas wherever whales might be living all over the world. Usually they stayed in the sea for about three years to catch whales.

The fights against the whales were very hard and required dauntlessness and the great courage. And the crews of the New England ships carried out this mission quite well.

EPISODE 7: Slavery

Phew.
This work never
seems to end.

Crack!

Arrrrr!

As they settled the new land, the first thing the settlers had to deal with was a shortage of workers.

The shortage was more serious in the South because its main crops, such as tobacco, needed many workers to be successfully farmed.

In the early days, European immigrant workers could handle all the work on the plantations.

There were plenty of people in Europe who wanted to go to America but could not afford the ship fare.

Many people moved to America this way.

And in some courts in Europe, a judge would ask the prisoner.

Prison or America?

If you choose to go to America, you won't be put in jail

America.

Muhahahaha! Good choice!

And sometimes children were kidnapped and sent to the plantations in America.

Also, advertisements that exaggerated the truth about America were used to attract people to work in the plantations in America.

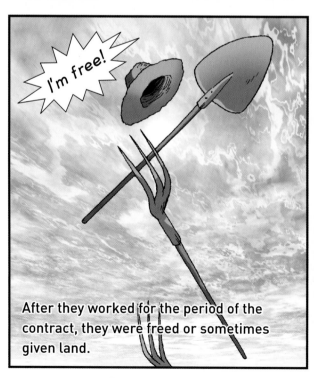

I'm free!

After they worked for the period of the contract, they were freed or sometimes given land.

Many of them became independent farmers, and some of them even moved up the social ladder to become colony leaders.

But in the 1660s there were fewer and fewer European workers, and the plantations in the South faced a serious shortage of workers.

Plantation owners used the slave trade, by which Africans were forced to come to America to work for settlers.

It was 1619 when Africans were forced to come to the New World for the first time.

A ship from the Netherlands landed at Jamestown with twenty Africans on board, and that was the beginning.

Following the introduction of slavery to North America, African slaves continued to arrive at a small but steady pace until the end of the 17th century when manpower and labor shortages in the South forced a massive expansion of the slave trade.

In the North, most slaves were given domestic jobs as maids and cooks and nannies.

Because of different economic structures, slaves were generally treated better in the North than the South, where manual labor was needed in great numbers to maintain the plantation crops.

Colonies in the Middle

The middle colonies located between the South and New England had relatively wide lands and fertile soil. So crops grew very well. Here, wheats were mainly produced, and barleys and ryes were farmed. Cows, lambs and pigs were also raised here. The farms in the middle were small-sized and self-cultivated. Of course, there were also some as large farms as those of the south.

Early in the colonial period, England waged wars frequently. When England waged wars against other countries such as Spain and France, the trades of the colonies were damaged severely. And the trade ships were changed into the pirate ships to make up for the damage.

The pirate ships, armed with weapons such as artillery, were permitted to seize the ships of enemy countries and to take property.
The pirate ships helped the British navy, and sometimes they gathered huge wealth in a day.

After the wars were over, some continued to work as pirate ships. In reality, many of the rich of the colonies gathered the huge wealth by starting off as the pirate ships.

EPISODE 8: We Want Self-Government

America started off as a colony of Britain, but the way of life there in the early days made it difficult for Britain to rule and control America.

Many settlers did not stay in one area (as they had in Europe) but lived scattered all over the continent.

They moved constantly in search of good land. In this way, they pioneered new settlements.

By overcoming difficulties, their pioneering spirit of freedom became a part of their thinking.

It was almost impossible for the British government to control the people, particularly in the farthest areas of the continent.

Remote towns that were totally out of British reach were called extraterritorial areas.

The Atlantic Ocean also made it difficult for the British government to use its power in the New World.

For all of these reasons, Britain's power in America grew weaker.

In the early period of American colonies, Britain was busy dealing with its own issues in Europe, and this kept Britain from paying enough attention to its colony across the Atlantic.

Away from direct rule by Britain, most colonies in the early days acted more like partners to Britain than subject.

The colonists in America felt very independent.

We are not meek.

We have our own power and independence.

In fact, some colonists were extremely hostile to Britain.

Pah!

I, King James II, will never allow that.

The power to rule over the colonies belongs to me, not to them.

However, the settlers' attempt at self-government was challenged.

King James II appointed Sir Edmond Andros as governor of New England, the northeastern area of what is now the United States.

As governor, he carried out harsh policies to punish those who resisted.

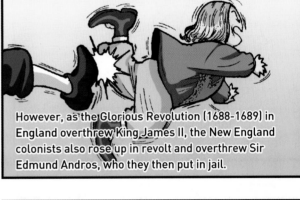

However, as the Glorious Revolution (1688–1689) in England overthrew King James II, the New England colonists also rose up in revolt and overthrew Sir Edmund Andros, who they then put in jail.

Yet the American colonists still did not have true self-government, as the British simply appointed new governors.

The Declaration of Indulgence, written in 1687, supported freedom of religion in Britain.

The British Bill of Rights, declared in 1689 on British royal power, placed a limit on British royal power.

And John Locke's writing deeply impressed the colonists.

John Locke said that government is not based on divine right but on a social contract, and that the people, who have natural rights, have the right to rebel when governments violate these natural rights.

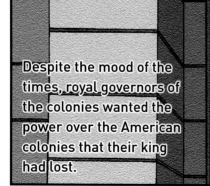

Despite the mood of the times, royal governors of the colonies wanted the power over the American colonies that their king had lost.

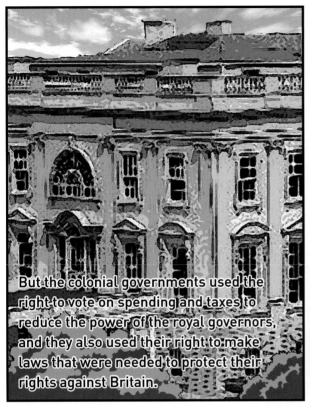

But the colonial governments used the right to vote on spending and taxes to reduce the power of the royal governors, and they also used their right to make laws that were needed to protect their rights against Britain.

The colonial governments continued to gain the right to govern themselves throughout these struggles with the royal governors.

The end result of these events was that power over the colonies moved from London to the capitals of each of the colonies.

The Tradition of Autonomy

The new continent was the colony of England.
Therefore the new continent had to be ruled by English kings and English laws.
But fortunately(unfortunately for England), the new continent was too far apart from England geographically.
In fact, it was almost impossible for England to control the colony effectively.

Furthermore, every colony offered much more privileges on the freedom of land ownership, inhabitants' autonomy and religion competitively to attract more immigrants.

And besides, as what the pilgrim fathers showed, those who came to the American continent had the yearnings for freedom in their hearts.

In addition, the people in the new continent were accustomed to making up their minds by themselves because they were living in a wide land unlike Europe.

Owing to these environments and traditions, inhabitants' opinions were gathered, public opinions were formed naturally, and finally, the tradition that they solved their life-related matters by themselves was set up.

The Bill of Rights and America

King James II, who came to the British throne in 1685, was a Catholic and he propelled the resurrection of the Catholic Church suppressing the Church of England. When James II attempted a tyranny oppressing the opponents who objected to his policies, the citizens roared with complaints.

Thus, the leaders of the parties, Tory and Whig were discussed in the Congress, and sent an invitation Duke Orange and his wife Mary to come to England and succeed to the British throne.
Duke Orange and Mary want to London with soldiers and succeeded to the throne in favor of their suggestions. Then the Congress submitted the declaration of rights to Duke Orange and Mary, and it was approved by them. Then they came to the throne, and became William III and Mary II.

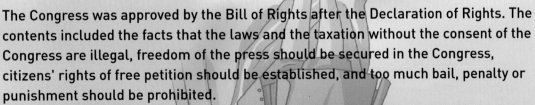

The Congress was approved by the Bill of Rights after the Declaration of Rights. The contents included the facts that the laws and the taxation without the consent of the Congress are illegal, freedom of the press should be secured in the Congress, citizens' rights of free petition should be established, and too much bail, penalty or punishment should be prohibited.
The Bill of Rights brought to an end autocracy and became the basis of the establishment of parliamentary politics. And it also affected greatly to the American people in the colonial period including the Declaration of Independence, Virginian Charter of Rights and Massachusetts' Declaration of Rights, etc., as well as to British people.

EPISODE 9: The French and Indian War

Britain and France had been rivals for a long time.

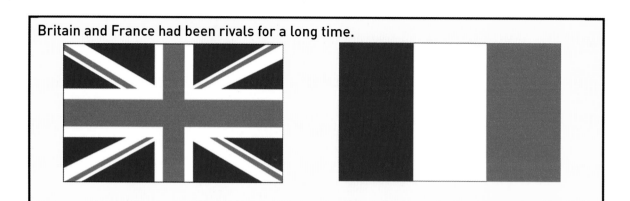

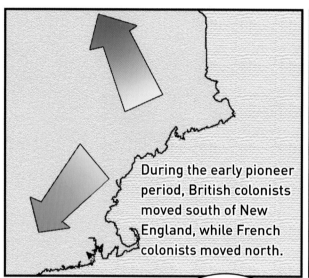

During the early pioneer period, British colonists moved south of New England, while French colonists moved north.

Clashes between the two nations began as each tried to expand and create more colonies.

We French want to move south where the weather is warmer.

Brrrr! It's too cold here. Besides the soil is very difficult to grow things in.

But the British settlers were also feeling as though they needed more land.

There are more and more immigrants coming to America every day. We're the ones who really need new land.

So we'd like to move to the West, but we can't...

...because the Appalachian Mountains are blocking us.

The only route we can take is under the control of France, so we can't go through.

The conflict flared up because Britain gave a colonial company the Ohio Valley.

For Settlers

The company began asking people to settle there.

France did not like this.

Pah!

That is ridiculous!

They don't really think that we are just going to sit back and watch them take our land, do they?

France sent its troops to build forts, threatening the new settlers.

Virginia militiamen (armed colonists from Virginia) were sent to fight against the French, but they were defeated by French soldiers.

The commander of the troops from Virginia was the twenty-two-year-old George Washington, who later became the first president of the United States.

The news of defeat arrived in Britain.

This could be a chance.

Why don't we shove the French out of the way?

Britain sent a large army right away.

So France joined forces with Native Americans.

Hey, my friend. We need to talk.

About what?

Well...

What? The British troops are coming to take our lands?

Then...then...what should we do?

No worries! We can join hands and crush them.

Great! I agree.

The relationship between the French and the Native Americans was friendly.

Because the French who came to America were mostly traders or hunters...

...they did not settle in one place and so didn't try to take the land away from Native Americans in order to farm.

Also, Native Americans made very large profits by trading fur with the French.

The first large military clash took place on June 19, 1755, at Fort Duquesne (which is now Pittsburgh).

Under General Marquis de Montcalm, the forces of the French and the Native Americans had victory after victory.

The British were losing in part because they'd been so busy with the Seven Years' War (1756-1763) in Europe that Britain had barely focused on the situation in the New World.

However, as the Seven Years' War was coming to an end, Britain sent well-trained troops to the New World, and this soon changed the progress of the war.

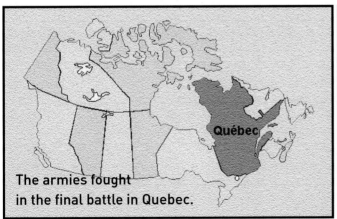

The armies fought in the final battle in Quebec.

The strong French forts of Quebec were not easy to attack.

But the British troops climbed a cliff behind the forts and made a sudden attack on the French troops.

The attack brought victory to the British troops, also leading to the victory of Britain in the French and Indian War.

The following year, the British troops finally conquered the last fort of the French troops in Montreal.

France promised to give up all of Canada to Britain.

The governor of Canada signed the surrender in which France promised to give up all of Canada to Britain.

England vs France

England and France were old rivals.
The two countries fought for the right
to rule the colonies in many places of the world,
and they also fought in America unexceptionally.

The beginning of the fight in the new continent was due to fur.
Lots of beavers inhabited the Great Lakes and St. Lawrence River and their quality
was superior, so they were very popular in Europe.
When the English government permitted the entry into this region, France got
became angry with it.

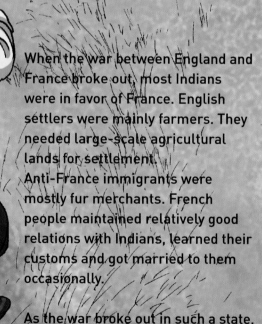

When the war between England and France broke out, most Indians were in favor of France. English settlers were mainly farmers. They needed large-scale agricultural lands for settlement.
Anti-France immigrants were mostly fur merchants. French people maintained relatively good relations with Indians, learned their customs and got married to them occasionally.

As the war broke out in such a state, most Indians were in favor of France.

Battle of Quebec

As the war between England and France progressed favorably for the French army, the British King George II sent a young and able General James Wolf to fight against the French commander.

The war began to be reversed under the direction of General Wolf, and they fought a battle which would determine the crucial result of the war in Quebec in September, 1759.

Though British army blockaded the St. Lawrence River and blocked the supply route, the fortress of Quebec was an impregnable one. They held the fortress against the enemy army's two months' attack.

However finally, British army found a narrow pathway in the western cliffs of the fortress, and 4000 soldiers climbed up the cliffs, and then they could attack French army and won the victory.

Quebec Battle was an unusual battle in which the two commanders-in-chief of both armies were killed, general Wolf and the French commander, and with this battle as a momentum, British position in North America was established firmly.

EPISODE 10: Britain's New Policies

Let's go!

With the victory of the French and Indian War behind them, the settlers began to dream of moving to the West.

Huh?

Better stop dreaming.

Who said they can go to the West?

The Royal Proclamation

Besides, it would be difficult to control the colonists who live too far west.

That is what the Royal Proclamation is for.

At that time, the British government needed a huge amount of money to make up for the expensive French and Indian War and to support their rule in their newly expanded land.

So Britain enacted a number of acts to raise money. There was the Sugar Act in 1764, which created a tax on the import of molasses.

Additional taxes were put on wine, silk, coffee and other luxury items.

In 1765, there was the Quartering Act, which required colonies to support the British troops who were stationed there.

And then they enacted the Stamp Act, which required all newspapers, licenses and other legal documents (such as contracts) to use stamps that would give money back to Britain.

Two years later in 1767, the Townshend Acts imposed taxes on other colonial imports, such as paper, glass, lead and tea that was exported from Britain to the colonies. This made the settlers extremely angry.

We want these acts to be abolished!

We won't accept these taxes that were created without our consent.

Right!

We will refuse to buy all products from Britain.

I agree to this boycott!

Following the huge boycott of British products, a group called Sons of Liberty organized a protest to resist British troops.

On March 5, 1770, the first clash took place in Boston, where excitement about reform and new ideas was strong.

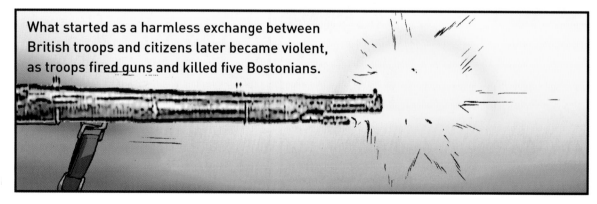

What started as a harmless exchange between British troops and citizens later became violent, as troops fired guns and killed five Bostonians.

Called the Boston Massacre, the event proved the tyranny of Britain and encouraged a lot of strong anti-British feeling among the already angry colonists.

The Dreams Disappeared

As the French-Indian war ended with British victory, the pioneers on the border shouted for joy. Because the fertile lands over the Appalachian Mountains would be expected to belong to them.

The pioneers on the border who dreamed of movement, fur merchants, fur hunters and land owners who secured lots of lands in expectations of the rise of land price were damaged severely by the "declaration law".

And many oppressive measures such as The Act of Molasses, The Act of Fort Expense Allotment, The Stamp Act and Townshend Duties were made consecutively. These measures encouraged people's anti-England feelings with the recession which the war entailed.

The colonial inhabitants didn't just endure British continuous oppressive measures. Because British measures which infringed on the colonial inhabitants' freedom were unacceptable to them.

The reason why people came to the new continent was the yearning for freedom, wasn't it? Then the British rulers attempted to take freedom away from them.

People arose again and began boycott campaigns against purchasing British goods. British officials, custom officers, and the merchants who purchased British goods were threatened by the colonial inhabitants. There was no exception to the anti-England campaign, and even elementary school students participated. In the meanwhile, the Massacre of Boston happened in March, 1770. The soldiers who had shot the inhabitants were brought to the trial, but they were found not guilty and set free.

People couldn't stand it.
The colonial inhabitants got angry much more, and the anti-England trend was irreversible.

EPISODE 11: The Road to Independence

After the Boston Massacre, there were no more serious clashes between Britain and the colonies.

But in 1773, the British government decided to help a British company, and in doing this, they angered the colonists.

At that time, the British East India Company faced a serious money problem—they had too much tea to sell.

The company asked the British government to create the Tea Act...

...which would allow the company to sell tea directly to the colonists instead of selling to colonial merchants.

Up until then, the tea trade had worked in this way:

First the East India Company brought tea to Britain and sold it to British merchants at a higher price than they had paid for it.

Then the British merchants sold it to the colonial merchants at a much higher price than they had paid for it.

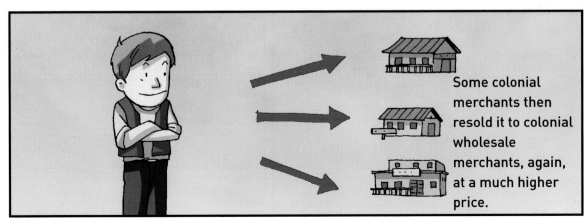

Some colonial merchants then resold it to colonial wholesale merchants, again, at a much higher price.

And finally the colonial wholesale merchants sold it to colonists at the highest price.

In other words, the tea went through four different distributors before it came to the colonial buyers.

| The East India Company | British merchants | The East India Company | Colonial wholesale merchants | Colonial consumers |

In fact, colonial merchants also smuggled tea into the colonies from the Netherlands and sold it for much less than the price of British tea.

By doing this, colonial merchants could make huge profits.

The Tea Act meant that colonial merchants could no longer have such big profits...

...because the East India Company could sell tea directly to the colonies and to the colonial merchants...

...and this meant that the company, by bypassing so many distributors, could sell the tea at an even lower price than the smuggled tea.

Colonial merchants had no way to sell the huge stockpiles of tea that they had stored.

If this continues, I will go bankrupt.

Well, I can't go down this way. Huh!

Colonial merchants joined hands with colonists, who were fighting for the independence of the colonies, by taking part in activities to resist Britain.

At every large port along the coastline of the Atlantic, the colonists gathered together to protest.

The British tea shipped by the East India Company was returned to Britain...

...or locked in storage so it could not be sold in the colonial market.

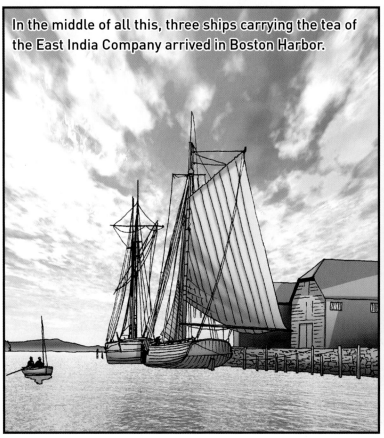

In the middle of all this, three ships carrying the tea of the East India Company arrived in Boston Harbor.

Although the citizens said they didn't want the tea, the company, with the support of the governor, tried to unload the tea anyway.

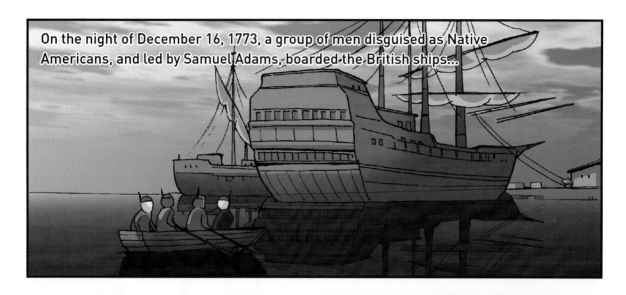

On the night of December 16, 1773, a group of men disguised as Native Americans, and led by Samuel Adams, boarded the British ships...

...and dumped the tea overboard into the water.

The incident is now called the Boston Tea Party.

The British government responded with stronger actions.

The Boston port will remain closed until you have paid the company back for all the dumped tea. Any gathering of people will not be allowed.

In addition, you must provide homes so British troops have a place to stay.

Also, lands from Ohio to the Mississippi River now belong to the province of Quebec.

The Quebec Act was another way to keep the colonists from trying to move west, and this naturally made the colonists even more angry.

In June of 1774, representatives of every colony except Georgia asked the king to put an end to all of these acts, which were sometimes called the Intolerable Acts or Coercive Acts, but the king rejected their request right away.

The first military clash between British troops and citizens occurred in Lexington, Massachusetts on April 19, 1775.

Eight citizens died, making the colonists even angrier than they had been before.

One month later, people from each colony met in Philadelphia to decide if they should wage a war against Britain.

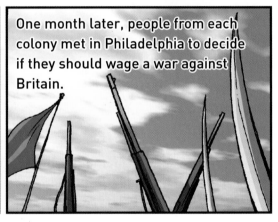

They decided that together they would organize a force to prepare for a war.

George Washington was appointed as the commander in chief.

On July 4, 1776, colonial representatives met again in Philadelphia, and all agreed to approve the Declaration of Independence!

This is how the United States of America came into being.
This is what the flag looked like in 1776. The thirteen stripes stand for the thirteen original colonies. The British flag in the top-left corner was soon replaced with stars, symbols of each state in the United States.

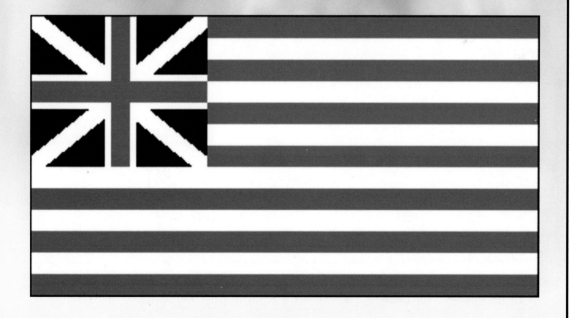

The commander of the British army in Boston where anti-England tendency was predominant was General Gage. He heard the report that the colonists were collecting ammunition and war stores in Concord, a few miles from Boston. He dispatched his forces and ordered them to confiscate the ammunition and war stores.

The British army arrived in Lexington early in the morning on April 19, 1775. Then it was the militia of 70 soldiers that was waiting for them. They were called "Minutemen" because they could be ready for fight in a minute.

The purpose of the militia was not to fight with the British army. They only intended to show their will and determination to object to the British oppressive rule. But the British commander saw the militia and got excited, and then he Oldered them to dismiss. The militia commander ordered not to fire his troops before the British army fired.

When the militia withdrew, a fire sounded. Then the British army fired a volley and the battle started. In this battle, eight militiamen were killed and 10 wounded.

Public opinion in the colonies began to roar. Now the war was not avertible.

After Boston Tea Incident, 12 colonial representatives, except Georgia, gathered and petitioned the British king for the repeal of 'the oppressive laws'. The British king's answer was "No".

On April 19, 1775, an armed conflict occurred between the British army and the militia, and eight American militiamen were killed. The English were not willing to yield anything and were sure that they could conquer the colonial inhabitants easily with armed forces.

But it was a miscalculation.
The feelings of anti-England were irreversible and even in Georgia where pro-England tendency was predominant, they came to call for independence gradually.

On May 10, 1775, soon after the Battle of Lexinton, the Continental Congress was held in Philadelphia. On May 15, the Continental Congress determined to go the war, and appointed George Washington as the first commander-in-chief of American army.

At last, the war for independence had begun.

Memo

Memo